Virginia Chase Sutton is, perhaps above all else, a poet of exquisite detail so that her precise and sometimes even obsessive attention to the seemingly mundane aspects of our objective reality come alive in her poems, and shimmer in the light of understanding. There is a sense too that these poems have come to us as if from a place very far away and full of mortal danger, as if the poet has rescued not only her own self from loss and despair, but language itself, so that the language throughout this highly accomplished first book is always fresh and vivid, the ordinary diction by which we curse and bless, love and hate on a daily basis, is resonant and restorative in its clarity and directness.

This is not the poetry of victimhood, but rather, the clear and necessary poetry of witness.

Bruce Weigl

Embellishments

poems by

VIRGINIA CHASE SUTTON

CHATOYANT

aptos, california

ISBN 0-9661452-5-9

Library of Congress Cataloguing-in-Publication Data
Sutton, Virginia Chase.
Embellishments / Virginia Chase Sutton
p.   cm.
0-9661452-5-9
PS3619.U72 E43 2003
811.54--dc21   2002114554

Cover art: *Orchids Need Humility,* mixed media by Catherine
Hammond.

Design by Susana Wessling

Published in the United States by
Chatoyant
PO Box 832
Aptos, CA 95001
www.chatoyant.com

Printed in the United States

Contents

Embellishments

To my daughters, Rebecca and Constance

Name the color, the one
you've been saving, memory's glimmering
spotlight and sequin...

Mark Doty

Chinese Robes

Because we were suburban schoolchildren
we thought one trip to Chinatown
would make us Chinese. Off the bus
and partnered, we wandered past storefronts

to a temple where the languid air was laced
with a fragrance that twined the collars
of our ironed shirts and dresses, hovered
around our little white socks, nestled between

shoulderblades that dizzy afternoon. We lunched
in a restaurant where food appeared in tiny
covered dishes and silver steam thinned above
eggshell cups. Captured by some radiance

we would not understand, we tried
to use chopsticks to anchor peapods
and water chestnuts into our wide and
empty mouths.

2.

My mother's jewelry box
is black lacquer, painted

with a small scene. Across
its wooden doors a Chinese maiden

bends her luminous neck, her heavy
coiffure of staggering black

plucked up with shiny hair ornaments
that waver across folding shoulders.

She waits for her lover beside
a pond. Open the doors.

Necklaces hang on racks,
a jumble of pirate treasure.

Mismated earrings clipped
to one another, pins and bracelets

in a wild grapple, like desire
while the girl's heart turns plum

beside the mirrored lake.

3.

The red silk robe unfolds,
  slipping from a nest of tissue paper.
    Gracefully, easily—it slides

into a tempting rosy puddle.
  A woman who loves me has wrapped
    the robe in white paper, color of mourning,

knowing that I do not love her.
  But the gown's astonishing flush
    is prettier than I have imagined red

could ever be. It matches her mouth.
  I recite true color of the body's longing:
    poppy, scarlet, vermilion, coral, crimson.

4.

We stroll through Chinatown:
my mother, father, sister, me.
Every outdoor shopkeeper calls to us.

We are perfect in this moment.
We examine bangles, boxes of incense
and brass burners, the tightly rolled

parasols still reeking of wax and oil.
Just past dinnertime, late summer, when
evening spirals the sky in a slow

incandescence. My fortune cookie says,
Your future awaits. My sister's
predicts, *Beauty is its own reward,*

while my father's reads, *Patience.*
Mother won't read her fortune to us
and has tucked it away in her cigarette case.

When a handful of firecrackers spark,
everyone claps. Is it a parade?
Could it be the sudden swish

of a dragon's head atop a wooden stick,
the legs writhing under a toss
of silk and mad color? My father

isn't fooled. Thinking the quick flares
are gunshots, he swoops Mother and my sister
to a doorway's safety. Alone on the street,

I see others have made the same mistake,
dropping to the street beneath the curb.
I watch the brilliant light stretch

along the sidewalk. I hold my new China doll
who bobs with each burst of fire.
Her rich cherry robes blister

into the melt of embroidered gold
chrysanthemums, her white legs and arms
dissolving us into the evening's end

where ordinary stars blot the night
in rippling waves of shredded silk.

Twisters

The sky is lovely: a sudden slur of night dropping
a furl of gray clouds that overlap until real color

is forgotten. Minutes ago the town's disaster alarm
rushed us to the street, loud pitch pulsing against
the drape of heavy air. Today's sky is astonishing,

the quick slide of night to mid-day, a greater sweep
of jade. Mother smokes, scans the dankness.

Muted green eases into sharp yellow, thickens
to a brushed patina. She's been in the basement.
Piece by piece, she's carted our furniture downstairs.

Now it's a big puzzle of tabletops, angled surfaces,
odd arms and legs. After dinner she leaves us

with her highball, metal ice cube tray, bourbon bottle,
cigarettes. From upstairs we smell the chemicals,
hear the steady scrub of steel wool, the drone of paint

transforming wood to antiqued avocado. Why is she doing this
under the gleam of the hanging bulb? Does she study

each piece, measuring the depths of shade against
hue? I sneak down to see the dining room table
stroked to a rich green, richer than its former maple.

Chairs are darker, olive, painted black over green,
smeared off at timed intervals. The bureau's

a failure, brightness of new spring,
too cheery. But the bookcases are perfect,
rubbed to the last stages of a bruise,

gentle as the moist color of sky seconds before
the twister hits. Mother's skirt rises with the wind.

Blue-green clumps of veins, small patterns
of light and dark. She studies the sky's turn to brine,
the thin slip of gray muting the rush of air and silence.

Only a week ago she drove me to the country
where a funnel slipped through farmland. We passed

police barricades parked at the edge of a stranger's property.
Caught in the twister's fierce logic, a house jostled
on its foundation, a car still parked neatly in its garage.

The barn flew across a field of new plants, ignoring
tossed beams and the scattering of wood. Mother said

the tornado came down from the west and we waited
until the clouds faded to a yellow poison. Today
she watches the dangerous sky whisk to the right shade.

She must need this heaviness, the sudden drop and scream
of inflated air, the silent shock of a funnel

that trips to ground for moments. It destroys,
jumps a block to fondle someone else's house, thins
and disappears, shredded to a ribbony vapor. She loves

the spindrift colors, saturated shades, the aching
triumphant spasm of green.

After the Wedding

we are kissing in his front seat,
parked at an all-night diner. It is raining.

My bridesmaid's gown of pink dotted swiss
lined in taffeta blossoms to a coil raised

above my waist. Across the street, my father
writes a check for my sister's wedding. Newlyweds

leave the hotel in a flutter of rice while over here
a wedding guest dips large fingers into my gown.

A plastic zipper opens, the boned bra unspans,
my glorious breasts fall into his hands. Unfamiliar

kisses, my mouth a circle of vodka and orange juice,
his a sheath of whiskey. Feet from the highway,

our bright skins startle restaurant patrons
who take another look through the windshield

as he palms my nipples to stubbled points. The bride's
bouquet, stuck in the steering wheel of his '63 Impala,

radiates white roses, pink daisies, baby's breath,
thin ferns misting with the car's every dip and wave.

Minutes, a sweet half hour. Damp wool traps his ankles,
a foam of dress and slip and legs billows over the seat.

A window's half-open, raindrops speckle our shoulders.
Headlights snap on as my father pulls out into traffic. Small

puddles break against this car where we spatter and moan.

Leaving

Someone is always leaving
before I'm ready. Years ago,
after a summer picnic, my mother

climbed into a smooth black tube
and stepped off a sandbar

in mid-Mississippi River. Red curls bleeding
across water, she skidded into the current.
She floated away on the edge of something,

skimming through afternoon light,
easing further down river and out of sight.

My father roared after her
in a borrowed boat while I wrote messages
in the sand with a thin stick, then let

my sister erase the words
with buckets of water dredged from the river.

Errand

Our sky is yellowing haze, a screen
of dark clouds, lights finally turning. My sister
is driving. She points to a crescent

lurking above a streetlamp. It hovers, banded
in reflective globes, rows of bulbs and spotlights,
muting afternoon into dusk. It follows us
down the block, lazing above old elms.
It turns when we do. We buy a gallon of milk,
butter, a pound of onions at the A & P.

We know it is waiting. Years ago, our mother loved
the scattered brilliance of candlelight. Evenings
she'd settle thick tapers everywhere: on the what-not shelf,

windowsills, bookcases. Friends sat in this light, hand
to hand, ouija letters arranged around the dining room table
along with yes and no. An empty highball glass
circled counter-clockwise, bumping letters into words.
On the couch, my sister hid beneath
great-grandmother's ochre afghan while I recorded

letters as the glass jittered. Sometimes, a glass moved
so furiously, it crashed. My sister surprises me tonight
when she watches the ship above the grocery store. It blinks

into a ripple of dead air. She finds a new way home,
dragging it behind us. I'm the one who's scared.
Lights skitter in no particular order, thin nail parings.
I tell her to speed up, hit the gas hard,
head for the police station, get witnesses,
don't trap us with this mystery. If it lands

before us and the road settles, easy
and quiet, will we stop, remove the keys, walk slowly
into a flurry of mirrors without ever asking? Her window's

shivered open, her brown hair light and dangerously beautiful.
She follows it. Lights blend to a wash of iridescent color,
crystal beads. We drive, my sister behind this spasm
of moon. Blissful, we pull to the highway
leading straight out of town.

Blackout

Even if I can't remember what came between
  midnight and dawn, I can see that night
cleanly, without clutter. I still see us

drinking gin and tonics before the dance.
  I surprise myself. The drinks are cold,
the way I like them, icy in a tall thin glass.

Gin is sharper than expected—after all,
  it was my mother's drink. As a child,
I vowed I'd never drink such bitter stuff,

crushed glass a glitter over her tongue.
  It turned my head. But this night,
I drink it with you, drink until the bottle's empty

and the mixer's no fun alone. Did you ask if I wanted it,
  or did we lift the bottle together, easy froth
of carbonation and clear alcohol? At the dance,

we drifted under a flashing silver ball, liking
  the way our feet stirred the air so close
to the floor. You brought more drinks

to our table. I drank until the evening hinged
  to a smudge. Later, someone said I tore
drinks from strangers' hands, the dance floor

a swirl of melting ice, a foam of alcohol.
  And somehow I can feel a barefoot stroll in a winter
garden, my toes a slow frost beneath our too careful

steps. Nothing. That's all. Unconscious until
   morning when I woke beside you in my bed.
I didn't need to ask, because you said *I loved*

fucking you. Again and again. I swallowed fast,
   leftover gin wrapping my tongue in an acrid wash.
Don't speak. Don't tell me what I know. *You were quiet*

for the first time in your life. You raised my legs,
   bowed me open with your body, touching
when I couldn't answer, kissing the flesh that never

loved you back, *Passed out cold. You didn't move.*
   What can I say tonight, that plummeting temperature
still a cloud of half-remembered surfaces? How

your touch hurts even now. That gin's a dream
   snapping me upright in bed some nights,
reminding me of the two of us wrapped

inside an ice-storm of blankets and sheets. How you
   took what you needed. How you never asked me
to open, but waited until the glass was empty

and I couldn't speak.

Constellations

Stars clutter our midwestern sky
around the night's soft bruises,
shadow evening with a watery vapor.
The bathroom light flickers, stuttering

as the fluorescent tube darkens. Neighbor boys
inquire about the messages that blink all night.
They count dashes and dots, Morse code
urgent in our second story window.

These secrets, my father says,
will never leave this house.
Sealed under every threshold and sash,
we cradle our safety behind curtains

rosy with ruffles. Mother sleeps
on polished sofa cushions in a wash
of urine, ice cubes invisible
under the coffee table. My sister's asleep,

dreaming of the nameless man inside our closet,
the one who whispers smoky memories.
I don't sleep. I think of stars,
how they blend into brightness

while the bathroom light unfurls its sweet staccato.
I never tire of the long inhalation,
the identical stabs of chalky light, the dullness
of night, a whole house sleeping.

Gardens

1.

Weekend mornings, alleys were wreathed
in the dazzling stain of color. Growers
from all over the state gathered their best:

chilled scents, heavily budded, any wild profusion
of flowers. My father's closed black truck
arrived downtown, stuffed with chrysanthemums.

How they unfolded when he flung open the rear doors
and allowed the blooms to crush into violet,
mauve, bronze. From the front seat, I'd look

past my shoulder to the spiky petals that pushed
our way to early morning. More trucks
crowded backstreets, each unloading fine crops

of floral offerings. Astonished flowers covered
dumpsters and loading docks with all their articulate
longing. I knew the secrets: the damaged had already

been discarded, shaken from terra cotta pots that waited
to be renewed. The shrunken, withering brown plants
had been displaced, readied for the dump.

2.

Mother planted spiced geraniums beside
　stepping stones, connecting our front porch

to the gravel driveway. Alternating salmon
　with a blushed pink, she trimmed patterns

in full sun. All those years working the greenhouse
　she still didn't know anything about flowers.

I knew she'd rather be behind the house where
　cramped sheaves of Lily-of-the-Valley puffed

white bells under broad green leaves. She'd fill
　cocktail glasses with those distended clumps, allowing

them to turn fretful and slick. Her favorite flowers
　were hyacinths; she loved the blossom's pulse

for one quick moment. Bulky spikes of those tiny
　flowers spewed dizzy fragrance, like the tester bottles

of *White Shoulders* and *Arpege* I touched
　to my wrist at the corner drugstore.

*   *   *   *   *

Lacy baby pink carnations twist into a corsage,
   bound by a flutter of white ribbons. She wears flowers

neatly pinned to her jacket's wide lapel. My father
   drives to Kentucky where they will be married.

They have known one another three weeks. Across
   state lines they won't need to lie about their age.

Under a busy trellis of tissue-paper roses, they agree
   to what is already lost, promises ended with a kiss.

In the judge's front room office, her wedding flowers wilt,
   scent vanished under the rooted knot of her perfume.

3.

Morning: someone must go downstairs and let in
necessary light. Heavy draperies run ceiling
to floor, patterned in an outmoded thirties style
with gigantic cabbage roses, long past their summer's
continuous bloom. Droopy petals are stung magenta, bile green

vines weave poisoned tendrils across the windowed wall.
One tug and the cord shushes curtains from their center,
opens the room to dawn. Dying bees lazily circle,
searching for a last way out. All night they've crept
down the chimney, dropped to the hearth, stunned

by the profusion of roses they cannot feed upon.
They've spent dark hours heading toward a petal's pleated
lushness, then fallen, unable to grasp the promised sweetness.

They circle, moving toward weighted roses that never
open as they work all night for some deliberate shelter.

I sweep the brittle shells away, not bothering to count
the hard bodies littering the carpet. I know there are people
who die from a single sting. These bees have fallen away
from flowers that are not full enough to hold them.

4.

My father talks to me of flowers.
He pulls an orange blossom from a branchy
desert flower in his yard, holds it to screen out

afternoon's last reflection. How can he know so much
about this plant, Bird-of-Paradise, its range of color,
habits, family, how it will live, how it changes shape

as it begins to die? As a child, I adored spring flowers
while it was still winter. We'd drive to the city
to walk gardens inside the Lincoln Park Conservatory.

At the door, a burst of air left us reeling as we inhaled
flowers forced into deliberate bloom. Color banked
at every turn and curve, extravagant tulips bending

near a fountain: *Mendel, Triumph, Cottage, Parrot.*
Singly and doubly petalled, top heavy on slim columns,
they collected in careful configurations. Mixed in

were trumpeted daffodils and narcissus in a showy lushness.
Persuaded into desire for one pastel moment, my parents
stood between landscapes of continuous and overlapping

color. Each spring they planned an arrangement of bulbs
while caught in this artificial garden. Then we drove home
to winter, knowing that whatever happened, it was simply

long past any bulb's time. So when we talk now
of flowers, I think of gardens. After Mother died, he sent
yellow mums, fisted bigger than any knots that might still

blossom. Seasons past, growing done. Apart from her
and yet he needed memory's stitched shelter. I planted
those mums in my backyard between garden roses that fire

into bloom just once each year. Neighboring tea roses
send out graceful buds and tight green leaves that I snip
in early morning, delicate and cool before the day begins.

But I wait for old roses. I need their limited passion,
their glory in that single instant when they flare
into a patient fullness worth waiting for, despite distance

and the careful losses that send me empty into summer.

Landmarks

Those narrow trees, stripped dead
and gathering radiance are what

I'll remember. Stranded in the lake's
center—their filigreed
tips shimmer over the flat water,

some kind of smoky blue glass.
That's what I always see first,

driving down the small hills
to Iowa City. Clipping around curves,
my black car is tight against the embrace

of yellow lines, then a quick spin
over the bridge. That fast and the trees

are behind us. We've come to forge names
on blank white sheets, a doctor's empty
pages. There's the drugstore

where we buy codeine cough syrup in dull
brown bottles. Can I explain the allure

of this stickiness as we open
our mouths to it? Heading north,
the man I thought I loved opens another

bottle, drizzles this sweetness over
his fat tongue. While I drive,

his heavy hands reach for me, and I let
the car shoot up then plunge down lazy hills,

a long slide into nothing but road
and repetition. *Watch for the trees,*
I tell him. From my window I see

their sudden sleekness, their splendid
bareness, the long trunks without clutter,
remote, upright in stagnant water,

unable to change.

Above the Beach

Though it's summer, we stand above the beach
in stiff winter dresses, dead husks of alewives
near our patent leather shoes. In the photo,

our home-permed hair frizzes
over the snap of small waves creeping
close to our feet. We are moving
to this new place, away from the lost business,

lost house, lost jobs. *In Chicago,*
Mother plans, *things will be different.*
But what do we understand this afternoon

about promises or journeys? It's lunch
at Howard Johnson's, Mother interviews
for a teaching job, Dad happy to be selling anything.
They rent the cheapest house, a flat green suburb

where we'll hide gallon liquor jugs in the trash
next year and the next. Gin bottles glint
against the moon behind the house. Upstairs,

we hide in our pinched room. A mirror image:
two pink and white beds, cartoon spreads, same
pink knit octopus squarely centered. In the middle
of the floor, we practice holding our breath.

Who will pass out, disappear into the rug's white nap?
There aren't any other sister snapshots. Just
this one, where two girls have been forced

to hold hands and pretend that their small faces
haven't been creased by the sun. On the beach
this afternoon they smell fish hulls,
piles of dead scales brushing closer with each wave.

Dad's Polaroid streaks the shot—bright
afternoon—so it goes into Mother's bureau drawer
with baby pictures, report cards, their wedding license.

I fish it out today to show my sister, wanting
her to see the two small girls, already
at arm's distance. She laughs at what we were
in our runover party shoes, dresses that barely button.

She knows what I do: the girls in this photo
already recognize that the sun's luminous gleam
won't shield them. It's what they cannot see.

Seaside Cemetery, Blue Hill, Maine

for my mother

Summering in Maine, we'd often walk
to the old cemetery that thrust out into the bay.
You'd carry a picnic basket through clumped
blueberries, trailing easily over someone's
mossy stone. Wild green waves flared, eroding
another's grave while your mother measured

the family plot. She showed us how with careful
planning, we would all neatly fit. The basket
was settled on your grandfather's grave. He was a judge
who prepaid a village laborer to sit beside his tomb
for three days, prepared to dig him up in case of sudden
resurrection. I remember your laughter wrapping

the silvery trees, how it carried out the tide to rocks
beyond shore. When I set down this gravel path
today, I want you buried here with your people,
ringed in the family name you honored the morning
I was born. It's been years since I sat
in a church, listening to someone who never knew you

confuse our names. My sister, your other child,
mailed your ashes to her house. She packed you
into a tall jar that perches above her kitchen
sink. Do you ever wonder why I couldn't claim you,
why you can't be here within the stone fence
that closes the family in? The last thing you said

a week before your death was to end the fighting.
So I abandoned you in Arizona where desert heat

leaches dirt to a fine silt that you never liked.
Let me imagine you here beside your mother.
Would you still argue, erect a stand of wandering
raspberries to mark with thorns your own separate

spots? Perhaps there's room near your father's
simple marker. Bare-handed, I clear brambles,
catch the sting of old vines that weave garlands
in this season over stones with half-remembered names.
Listen Mother, some afternoon, some summer day
sweeter than any other, I'll stake this place for you.

It won't matter that you're not really here. I know
you remained decades ago after one kiss pressed
to the monument centered in this plot. You even cried
a little. Surprised that you could mourn, I offered
my tin bucket of berries. Then I stepped back to let you talk
to the dead in any dreamy language that you could.

Perfume

for John

I bought scented soaps last week,
our daughters touching the soaring curves
of molded yellow seashells and blue swans.

They traced fingers over grooves nicked
into open flowers, fanning petals,
small sprays shedding some pale scent.

I wear perfume as I always have,
a curl of vines and knotted buds circling
my neck and wrists. My odor

is unchanged, no matter what else seems
to slip away. Roses still flower in the yard,
their thick colors blurring in a coil of night air.

It gathers outside our bedroom window.
Will you let the flushed bougainvillea drift
over our bodies tonight, remembering its impossible

sweetness? We made love for hours on the night we met,
in a dirty bed in someone's extra room. Your long body
stretched beside mine, rich kisses filling my mouth,

new words neither of us understood. Through the smudged
window, we saw a summer moon grow more yellow until
gold washed us to the back porch. We stood, our rumpled

bodies wet and weirdly supple under that half-light.
Can we recall all the places we loved? In the blur of so much
time, I remember how your hands reached for me, even

in the dark. Stay awake awhile. We will trail our hands
beyond this heaviness, spin scent into another night.
Our bed's overrun with fragrances we won't name.

Family Meals

1.

Counter or booth, the hostess asks.
Every Friday when Dad's off the road,
we come for a family dinner.
Our regular booth's by the cigarette machine.

The food's lousy: runny spaghetti sauce,
chunky iceberg, tomato on the side.
Orange sherbet in metal cups hurts our teeth.
My sister stirs hers to soup, swallows it down

with a spoon. We've lost our manners. We girls
push through double glass doors, wait
under a neon sign. We like this everyday food
so much, my father steps in other nights for bags

of turkey sandwiches. Once, we shuddered them down
in our greed and soon lost that gray sliced meat,
pretty foamy bread, in a wash of choking and trembling.
Mother followed on all fours, drunk, scouring stains

as we crawled up the stairs. Back at the restaurant
the next Friday night, we return to our safe booth
a bit diminished, and order the evening's special.

2.

Mother says cold beverages
are unhealthy. So we drink

room temperature milk, tepid water
right from the faucet. She tells us

of a late summer picnic twenty years ago
when her cousin drank too many sodas.

The whole family grouped one limpid afternoon,
billowed blankets and cloths over granite,

a sentimental occasion of cousins and
finger food. Betty and Mother sat beside

a stream that quietly rearranged soda bottles
glinting bluely underwater. It moved

almost too fast, bubbling the thick bottles
that waited, wedged between rocks. Betty

reached for another soda, *her third,*
Mother says, and cut her hand on a broken bottle.

The steep edge of glass split between her fingers,
and the chilled water slowed blood to mud.

She raised her arm. *Put it back,* Mother warned.
The soda? Betty asked, puzzled and fascinated

by the spill of ruddy drops over her burnished lap.
A local doctor stitched her up, matched skin

and muscle. But Betty never spoke another word.
Mother remembers the random stares, the stunted

hand's thick bandage over curvy black stitches.
Betty just dropped her other hand, Mother says,

into a rummage of rock and frigid water.

3.

It's barbecue weather, my father explains
out on our patio where bricks are slipping
from their irregular mortar. I'm just a kid,
barefoot, in shorts, helping him adjust the grill.

Always remember: six minutes on the first side,
turn, then seven more. His formula for steak
means a marbled pink interior in a striped
black shell. *The coals must be just right.*

Ashes fade to cream as the black declines.
Tap one and see the frenzied red core. I never
spot the skittering coal beside the grill
or feel the pain when my foot splays across

that heated surface. Later the burn will fester
and puff. But for now I know I'm passing
some test, of walking barefoot and sweaty
over new coals, keeping my careful silence.

This Summer's Peonies

Everything in this room is a scummed surface
needing to be washed: metal rims,
plastic mattresses dotted with grated airholes,
molded furniture of textured plastic. *Nothing*

is beautiful here, my mother mumbles, all tears.
Her room's a clutter of walkers
and wheelchairs, privacy curtains never
drawn shut. I want to lie, to say

I visit often. My arms are filled
with clusters of this summer's peonies.
I've wrapped their silky stems in a bandage
of wet napkins to keep them fresh. How these flowers

puff into layers of rounded petals, each center's
faint knot foaming to the richness of pink
or lavender! Pale fragrance scents my hands. Dirt
bruises my palms, these stems and petals taken

from bushes in the side yard. Put them in a jar.
Let them billow over thick glass, shed their color
across plastic and disinfectant. Two old women
snore above the fretful hiss of catheters.

As their urine slowly rises in plastic bags,
it darkens to umber. Mother doesn't sleep at night.
She tells me smudges of hallway light drift
through the open door when the orderly arrives.

It's time, it's time, she whispers. The tube
in her nose cramps its way down her throat
and the machine clicks off another feeding.
Cloth diapers gather between her thighs, glow

sweetly beneath the warmth of clear urine. She needs
to be changed. He's all the way in. They listen
to the old women moaning behind their empty mouths.
Do the women dream of desire, of rolling over?

Who could imagine the beauty of this gesture?
Mother's eyes slip shut, the only movement left.
His hands, she says, *his hands.* Now he eases down
bedcovers stamped black in blocky letters, pushes aside

the gown marked with her first name. I can still
hear his fingers paint her nipples to points,
how his hands flutter and break against her skin.
It's over in minutes, this touching, never enough,

yet always more than she wants. When I ask
What is his name? her stiff white arms
roll up against her chest, flatten her breasts.
Forgotten muscles spasm into memory,

everything she has lost. *Take a breath.*
Inhale this odor of old bodies, of flesh rotting off
the bone, of skin needing touch, of soft convulsions
and lush summer flowers bending in a castoff jar.

Desire

Miles across this unfamiliar town,
my father is dying, his stripped heart
shattering under layers of old habits.

In the room next door, I know my sister's husband thinks
of marking stiff motel sheets with our stained
kisses, the dark black plum of desire. Last night,

we watched my father's shimmering pulse,
how oxygen blushed his skin into gray satin.
Too weak for talk, he waved one big hand,

rotating the palm like a broken religious figurine
with its incomplete blessing. *Your father wants this,*
my brother-in-law whispered at the all-night diner

over hamburgers and beer. He talked about my sister,
shut up back home with our invalid mother,
of the cars he'll someday buy for her, acres

of chrome and suede that equal love. Just last week
she said: *Promise. You'll never sleep with my husband.*
And I did. How easy to taste his open mouth,

the dull gentleness of his long legs, the simple
turn of his ordinary hips. When he's back
in his room at night, he calls home to tell her

what she asks to hear. And my father is getting better;
his heartbeats melt to a slow crawl, his legs
drifting inches from the floor. If I open the door

and call to my brother-in-law tonight, will anyone
remember? Will anyone have to know how his hand
lifts my skirt, if I ask him to fumble toward my skin,

the tender mauve and gold beneath it? Because it's late
and the door between us is only veneer, I promise I won't
raise my voice above this sigh. Just one breath. Listen

to new hearts, moving all over town.

In the Fitting Room

of this swanky lingerie shop, a girl
is learning all the possibilities

of desire. An elderly saleslady offers
instructions, tells her how to bend
and shimmy her breasts into the bonded

stiffness of the lace trimmed bra.
It doesn't fit. But the girl loves

the tiny crimson appliqué rose, hidden
like a blush between the cups, small
as a secret. The bra's band has tightened

until each breath is cut in half, sharp
as the snap of taffeta. Her new breasts

rise above the crackling fabric,
luminous ovals unwilling for this,
or any kind of confinement. Her mother sighs,

hating the rush of half-grown roundness
gleaming above her daughter's body. How

she scorns this turn to flesh, the thickening
of arms and belly, the thighs spilling flesh.
She has watched and watched the slow boil

of her daughter's skin, this baby who only
grew fatter. She propped bottles against

the infant's small chest, formula washing down
in torrents. Drained and emptied. But the mother
doesn't know what the girl realized years

ago: it was either swallow or drown. Now
the mother's cigarette has narrowed to a butt.

Everyone looks in the mirror. The artificial
pulse of spandex and rubber mixed and tugged
beneath the mother's sensible wool suit is all

that keeps her upright. The saleslady
unfurls her measuring tape, refigures numbers

and disappears. Dizzy with secret gluttony,
the girl thinks of all the men who will try
to capture her breasts beneath their large palms

or perhaps skip a breath while trying to swallow
them whole. She hopes her blowsy pink nipples

will spray them with the heavy scent of sweet
blue milk. And all of this is to come, she thinks,
admiring the swelling high above the fabric

never designed to contain such lushness.
Her skin is glazed beneath discreet

fluorescent lighting. The girl ignores her mother;
that worn body has been tightened and lifted
for so long that it's turned hollow inside.

She looks instead at the flaring of handfuls,
armfuls of flesh. She's still growing.

Dissipate

No matter what I remember, I know
I'd ride my bicycle to a vacant house,
lingering afternoons in that tranquil Georgian
with impossible angles and square rooms,
a caretaker, I thought, while waiting for something
to happen. I imagined everything,

my tight-skinned body barely scattering
into blood. It was no surprise when a boy
climbed in an unlatched kitchen window,
wanting to show the luxurious melt
of hips and arms. Upstairs, I abandoned him
on the other side of a bedroom door, his hard hand

rocking the brass knob, his faint promises of knots
our varnished skins could thread, what love really is.
Outside my window, tall lilacs teased the ledge
with compact buds, so thick with fragrance
I couldn't see the ruin of sharp twigs or the brush
of his vague footsteps leaving me behind.

A year before, I stole a filigree compact
from my mother's dressing table, pretending it was mine
all along. One glossy click and its cloudy mirror
sharpened the contours of my face, another click,
fine powder lacing the glass against light.
Clasping gold edges in my palm, I gathered a slow pinch

of skin, nearly slipping away. And later still,
in bed with a stranger one sweet afternoon, twilight hours
of long, empty love, our bodies sinking across
a white wash of sheets, I remembered that boy
and how I would have been his lover
if he'd just turned the knob another way,
and I would have given back the compact, but she never asked.

My Mother Spontaneously Combusts
at Marshall Field's
& Richard's Swirl Shoppe

We're on our way to Better Dresses, her cigarette
spewing hot wind above teetering steps. She parks
me on a velvet stool then spools through racks
of suits and one-piece dresses. *The booze just*

packs it on, she complains to a manicured saleslady
before stepping into fine wool or rough silk
over her widening hips. After the stroke she'll
be tied to a chair in a slippery hallway, white straps

centered over thin breasts. Calling my father's
name, all night, one syllable sticks between her teeth.
Now we're searching the Boutique for a party gown
when I notice sequined smoke misting above

her curls. Chiffon panels foam under her cinched
bustline as she gives a model's twirl before a three-way
mirror. *Which outfits to buy today?* Downstairs
in Cosmetics, cool salesgirls too polite

to comment on the trail of ashes behind us offer
carafes of perfume for the wrist, pancake foundation
in thick glass bottles, mascara tubs she can spit
into. Next year, she's snapped into a rayon housedress

with slashed pockets, roomy cotton underpants
tugged to her ribs. Then I'll prop her in a chair's corner,
stuffed with dry grass and tinder scraps. Will she
buy me something now? In the parking lot she says,

When you lose the weight, I'll invest in pretty clothes.
Then it's your turn. Now it's mine. At the beauty salon,
a plastic cape drapes my belly. Short bangs. My hair
clipped to the neck, a new razor iced steel. Shaved

for surgery, her iron gray hair bristles to a crewcut.
I steady an auburn wig on her skull but it slips sidesaddle.
One chair over, red curls frost her face, pulled
from a baking hairdryer. Pink rollers. Silver clips.

Now I smell the burn, singed hair unmistakably blackening
each tender twirl. She bends her sleek neck to the mirror,
doesn't see the crack of fire spitting into glass. I watch
my reflected face, my plain smock, my smarting eyes.

She reaches for another cigarette. Bronzing lips steam into a smile,
dumplings boiling on the stove. Wait awhile. Some fires
smoulder before they explode. It takes time, I remind
myself, liking the operator's curling iron as it teases
gathering smoke into a nest of full flame.

The Barbara Adkins
School of Dance

The costumes we wore each spring
on the high school stage
were artifice I only now understand.
The year we were cowgirls in yellow satin,
we tugged on skirts that inflated

above our pale knees into a flurry
of scarlet tulle. When the house lights
went down, I swear that audience
swallowed one huge bright breath,
then exhaled in languorous wonder

as our neon lariats snaked in lazy eights
over our heads. I was almost afraid.
What was that breathlessness but some level
of passion, some kind of transformation?
My sister and I were reinvented each week,

students in a basement ballet school
that promised only that our parents
would have Saturday mornings to themselves.
Our endless forming and reforming
of positions and postures, the soft kid slippers

scissoring over a parquet floor—
that wasn't art, but desire. We were never dancers.
In black leotards, we practiced
the difficult steps we could never recreate
on our own. It was purely imagination

sending us into brave leaps and turns above the barre.
At home, our parents sighed upstairs
in their single beds after hours of longing.

Later, my father said it was only lust between them,
never any exchange other than just

the body. We grew up. What I remember clearly
are those costumes, glittering shells
we could slide into, leaving the ordinary behind
forever. Once we were ballerinas
in dusky purple tutus frosted and festooned

with silver beading and trim. With hair skimmed
from our round faces, our rhinestone crowns
nodded to the music. The last recital,
we were Vegas showgirls. We squirmed
into one-piece outfits, almost like bathing suits,

but with style. Spangled draperies
extended floorlength, this casual brush
against dirt and elevation. Wristbands of sequins,
veiled turbans, melting diamonds and finery
fluttered as we toed our masking tape marks.

What I see now is not precision but a wavering line
of schoolgirls of staggered heights
and mismatched bodies. But each season,
we were netting the gaudy pearls, hips swathed
in turbulent black satin. What could we do

but rise? Our bodies shimmered
tiny ice chips, velvets, flashy fabrics,
all display. I see now the meaning behind
those careful dances was all design, glaze,
random dazzle—the only hope we knew.

Embellishments

Mother called it mutilation.
  As the needle swirled across the template
shooting gaudy Christmas color,

I knew it was right. Consider the pain.
  Never mind the fine curl of silvered needles,
clean, sterile. The bite and stain forever

on the skin. Or staring men who fan behind
  the artist's tints, his colors pulled from mixing
bowls and pans, primary hues of all his longing.

Whiteness. Deep bitter blue veins. My breasts.
  A slur of candied red, darkly green apple,
a smudge of summer yellow over black corners

already sketched. All that desire: rows of men
  watching my naked breasts, their pocketed hands,
rub of hips in unison, my steady gleam under

a lamp's small focus. I grow beneath his touch.
  Spilled circles increase their glow, pale pink
raspberries, erupting nipples after the crush

of his hands. To be wanted by so many men.
  To long for shifting hands, the body tightens,
fine lines tallied before the gushing glut

of color that filled each individual petal
  and leaf. As a child, I saw Mother rise
over a stranger's back. Her legs opened

and cracked as she stretched behind him
  on his motorcycle's slippery bench. They
embraced, her manicured fingers twined about

his waist. No smile or wave. Just a straight line
  to the corner. Twisted in ornate darkness, the scent
of night-blooming flowers and a bit of air stirred.

Afterward, she limped to the kitchen and buttered
  the new burn on her right leg. It was
a perfect circle, a cookie cutter cutout

forever melted into skin. She stroked butter
  back and forth, trapped heat way down.
Raised bubbles, little kisses,

boiled to the top. She was marked by that
  translucent ride with a stranger through
an empty town. Her skin took it all, healed

dark, blossoms of red and pink dripping brown
  and yellow. Tattoos scab, and when mine was picked
away, colors were raw, sharper than a scar.

Is it a pierce, stain, wound, cut, slices
  of body dragged into a scar or scab?
Mother never said which touch is truest. We're

so alike. I still tingle to those tiny kisses,
  explosions turned to oil, spoiled skin, permanent heat
all the way down to the bone.

Hotel Rio

Consider this summer evening, so hot
we punch on the air conditioning as soon

as the metal door unlocks. The gold shag's
pared to a whisper from too many transients

who've marked each surface with their stubbed
cigarette burns and cocktail hour rings. This

is a place for drunks and lovers who can afford
only an hour or two of madness. He pulls the faded

avocado quilt to the floor. White sheets already
dim to a tepid gray beneath the swag lamp's

solitary light. Undressing, he folds his clothes
in careful geometrics, their dull shine an ache

I already imagine pushing in the dark slit of my belly.
I turn the bathroom tap to cold, rinse out a thin cloth

to wash. Silver paint peels from the bathroom's
muddy mirror and the soap I'm unwrapping smells

of gardenias. I'm drunk enough to remember
each minute with him tonight. My white flesh gleams

in the murmuring mirror. Does it reflect only
what passes before it? Sheets wad below his body.

Nothing about this stranger's embrace
is easy, although it is everything I've told him

I desire. The hard rise of his body lengthens,
our bodies turn and slant until we spill in the fit

of wanting. Spasms of summer storms
are waiting, waiting. His legs are sticky, clinging

like wet paper to my belly and breasts. It's over.
Now he's in the shower rinsing away sludge and sweat

and the silk of my mouth. Alone on the mattress,
my thighs are open and wet. What do I want

from him? When he's finally dried off and dressed,
trailing the faint pulse of wedding flowers,

I will ask him to kiss me goodnight.
Cold air blasts from the window unit, the chill

settles all along the bed's damp pools. Outside,
I know that concrete streets tarnish under the slow

gathering of clouds and the constant throb of bubbling
air. I'm spinning. This room just gets colder.

The Rink

The skating pond's perfection frightens us,
too used to snowbanks, shoveled walks,
the careful grip of sand and salt.
One ruined evening before Christmas,

Mother's decided we should learn to skate.
Contrary in winter coats, hats fastened
to our glassy heads, we exchange ordinary boots
for skates. Her breath is a fog of silver gin

pulling us to the pond's measured surface.
I can't stand up. My sister embraces a wooden snow fence,
my father is a sculpted shadow on a bench. Mother
is porcelain, blooming across the rink's
frozen shimmer. Last year, our cat climbed

the Christmas tree. Branch by branch,
we heard the tree's soft give as he moved
through shivering beads, his careful paws
reaching for spangled tinsel. On the highest
branch he shifted, rode the tree down. Ornaments
clattered into mosaics, sequined fancywork

smashed across the hardwood floor. I still see
the suspended perfection of a pink teapot,
a metal drum, each wavering glass ball.
My mother cried at the sweeping up
of what once held shape, the dashed glitter
of painted exteriors, silvery interiors

simmering in a dustpan before it was all tossed away.
This Christmas I want to stay awake all night
under the tree's plain white lights
beneath the comforting drift of falling needles.
Don't I get everything I ask for?
It's the giving up I don't understand. Consider
Mother, drunk in a Pucci hostess gown

while my father chooses a sensible tree
in the Elks Club lot. Our lists dwindle
each year, the asking done, toys safely

selected. Am I really thinking of this
on the frigid rink, my legs collapsing
into the frosty tuck of wind?
Now she pushes off on white skates,

the chill flash of blades threading her
toward the caress of darkness.
See the precise patterns, the ripple
of the very drunk, how her arm reaches
through memory to drift into this sequence
of spinning and vague shadows etched on ice.

Night Terrors

1.

It's the light that wakes me each night: a smooth triangle widening over the bare floor as the door quietly hinges and Mother's big body eases all the way in, ribboning the light to shadows. Her flat white face glimmers along my bed's blanketed edge, amber fumes of bourbon sift through her teeth. *Listen,* she says, *I never wanted a daughter.* Her breath burns my eyes. *I know how you are: lazy and selfish, asleep when I need you.* She can spin the words for hours until her voice blurs into the sounds I never recognize as my own tears. She backs out the door, carrying the last of the light as she leaves.

2.

On the forty-seventh day her eyes open within a soft corner of sleep. Someone is calling the same four syllables across hazy sheets. She cannot place the room: the man who mouths, two girls lining the bed's metal chill. So I glide thick curtains from a window, needing more morning in this tight room crowded with plastic pouches, pitchers, and basins. *I never wanted a mother,* I whisper to her reflection in the streaked glass. *Go ahead, sleep.* She drifts over our scrubbed faces, strange light mottling her skin. And word by word, she shudders back to sleep.

3.

A strand of Christmas lights flickers at the window, soft pastels ice our bed. My daughter lies squarely between us in a warm footed sleep. I roll to my side, giving them room. *What's wrong, wake up,* I call into her small ear. *Do you know me?* But her face is fisted shut, she cannot hear my voice. Yet as she moves to find me, her hands catch and flail in the empty center, darkness pinning us into one another.

4.

Talk to her. Maybe she can hear you, nurses instruct. *Who knows what's left of her now?* They smear more jelly into her fixed, dilated eyes, staring beyond everyone at pleated curtains. She no longer blinks. All afternoon I watch her flat face, the long tear etching an arc from left eye to chin. I wipe it away with my palm, wonder if I should tell old stories again, remind her of everything lost, what she's working to forget. At dusk, her shallow breath sharpens, pointed toward stars just rising outside this window. They push her toward last darkness. *Sleep deeply enough,* I warn her, *so nothing will wake you for what is left.* I sit back and wait for morning. I think of how I will remember this, now that there is nothing left to do.

Tia Maria
and Blue Sugar Cubes

I never planned to kiss your careful throat
or the sweet small nipples of your breasts.
A woman, I said, *will never get me*

in bed. But you walked me down that slash

of winter highway after my lover abandoned me
at the bar. *I'll see you home,*
come with me, you promised. And above purpling sheets

that plumped your bed, you pulled me down.

Our legs were a better fit than ever I imagined,
the gloss of winter into white, the slow move
of my body to the bed's round corners and back

to the center of your unforgiving hands. *Touch me*

sang a voice—yours or mine? It was my mouth, a warm melt
into your smile. I see our small table, still and perfect,
a haze where we drank Jamaican coffee that night. We sucked

sugar cubes that were flared blue moments before,

the alcohol a faint flicker above cream.
I watched your blonde hair tendril,
your face tipping mauve against a cigarette's crushed light.

And this is important, Joanne, you thawed my icy hands

against your flushed mug, the coffee soaking amber
in the mix of liqueur, the slick of whipped cream.
More sugar cubes dissolving under our tongues,

blue kisses. I remember walking a freezing road,

our voices a polished curl in the sharp night air.
Who heard our tremble, our skid over thick ice, our crash
into that lovely white snowbank? And if I really remember

anything the way it was, it would have to be your hands,

their knowing slide to my glazed fullness, the heavy hang
of my breasts and hair over your shoulder. If I
could say anything now it would be how sorry I am

that the one night I tasted a storm of cold road

and the break of your longing, I could only wake
in the morning and tell you I hadn't wanted it.
The Tia Maria had washed me to your face

and tongue. Those burnt-sugar flames

rising above sharp liqueur melted my lips.
Vapors of cream couldn't hide my intoxicating swill
of drink after drink, fire and color, shot silk,

the savory slur of desire.

At Yellowstone

She slid into the car's vinyl front seat
clutching a pan of bacon that still sputtered
greasy rivulets, held at a safe distance from her face.
Mother locked the door with her elbow.
I was hidden in the backseat,
reading in the day's last dusky light,
astonished by the pan and Mother's hair
slipping under her paisley headscarf. *The bear,*
she whispered. And there was the bear ambling
toward our fire, a large group of campers
following along. It flipped open our cooler,
buried a paw in margarine, snuffled around
for something greasier. It turned toward the car
and the bacon, easing up on hind legs, pressing its big paws
flat against Mother's window. She beat
on the closed glass with her metal spatula,
drops of translucent bacon fat arcing into the backseat,
protecting the pan with the terrified curve
of her breasts. The bear, I remember, was small.
Its brown face seemed tired, painted
with spit and dirt. Later that night,
my father drove us to a trash dump
down a long broken road to wait for grizzlies
who feed on everything campers leave behind.
By flashlight, inside the car, we watched them
tear bags and cans with one simple movement
of their large gray paws. *Now that's a bear,*
my father said clearly, admiring their size
and relish of garbage as superior.
Leaving the park the next morning,
they both rolled down their windows to feed
puffy white marshmallows to young black bears
that begged and mugged alongside us all the way out.

Raft

Down a small hill etched by a long-ago glacier
  tonight's water gleams, a shimmer of lead and silver.
    On this bit of sand, nearly a beach, we leave

our summer clothes. Halfway to the raft, I stop,
  tread water, my hair snaky clots dripping over
    my plain whiteness. You wait for me, your hair

almost black, your body glazed in shadow. After the long drive,
  my husband's asleep in the small square bed, one sheet
    wrapped around his narrow body. He dreams and drifts

over a pillow we've brought from home, small blue flowers
  pale beneath his cheekbone. Moonlight spins us to the raft
    and up the slender ladder. We remember the same swim

five years before with Annabelle, the Scottish
  mother's helper from next door. Our skins flickered in
    and across the surface, an arm or breast just breaking

water. Who was more beautiful? Whose arm did you want
  around your throat? Our hair tangled, our shoulders
    bleached in moonlight so sharp we closed our eyes to it.

A hand reached for me, felt my waist, carefully inched
  around a breast. I was floating, you and Annabelle
    ferrying me to the raft. When the man next door

snapped on his floodlight, black beads of water
  quickened to gold. He tossed snowballs, frozen,
    snowpacked, at our phosphorous bodies, ice carefully

stored from last winter's hardness. They melted our flesh,
   star-shaped, not nearly round enough, twinkling
      into transparent circles at the lake's cool bottom.

Now we feel the rough planks beneath our naked skins,
   stars clustering your eastern sky, more brilliant
      in this country. I touch my head down, smell the powdery

texture of too many days in the sun. Why did you wait
   until now to ask to touch me? Why do you ask now,
      in this stillness, when I can only say no? Why do you

want this melt of our bodies this evening—to give me
   the child I've been needing so long? And in the morning,
      your lake is still dark, the raft only a small distance

from shore. In full day I see the pearl-edged water
   break against the raft's cracked boards, keep moving,
      form and reform. My husband is swimming across the lake,

nearly to the other side. We stand and watch
   his fine dark head slip underwater, then break again
      as the summer air softens and chills.

Amphetamines

All the way home heaps of dead leaves smolder,
the lacy smoke pressed to the pavement, sweet,

acrid, as my rushing heart empties small fires
in a quick slap of blood. Does anyone

hear its terrified beats, its rich dullness
as I walk over the last leaves? Down the block,

Mother snaps on a lamp, loving the brilliant beating
that shoves her toward night. It helps her fry

pork chops in a metal pan over high heat, sprinkle
translucent celery with a strangely steady hand.

But my heart on these pills turns hungry. Minutes ago,
up the street in a small office over the bank

Mother's doctor weighed and measured me.
Then he compressed my new breasts with slick hands,

nudged the buttery gleam of my hips with his body
on top of his elegant, cold table. Walking home,

I count capsules with blind fingertips, touch
the amber case he squeezed into my obedient hand.

I breathe the colorless dark, clutch my shirred heart
with my left palm. Pills make my body want to run home.

Instead, I barely push into our icy front room
where the dropping temperature presses my throat.

I'll share this cloudy bottle with her
after the doctor calls to report inches and pounds.

I count out the pills needed for the simmer of calories
and fat. Maybe she'll explain how the body works

harder this way. Maybe she'll open her bottle
of pills, dribbling a slow spill that shivers

dreams of honed cheeks and anklebones to our laps.
Methedrine. Dexedrine. She tells me to slip them beneath

my glittering tongue. I endure the melt, a slow dissolve,
mouth and heart curdling against the quick backwash

of blood. Dinner's on the table. Full plates
hiss a warning, our watchful hearts buzzing.

Measure a careful portion, wait for the doctor's
remedy, the swell of clean pink hands.

Falling

I've never been with you
 before the fall, when the body
  rises and rises, erasing touch.

You tell me sensation quickens,
 weaving in the luster of entire seconds
  before nothingness. Then your body

slips its skin, transforms, and hits hard.
 Curled into a metal desk, you're writing sums,
  pinned with other boys in a classroom.

The day's lesson wavers across the blackboard,
 figures floating in a strange wash of rhythm.
  That first time, the desk pinches hard

then dashes you to the floor. Waking up
 in the ambulance you said, *I remember,*
  I remember. Each time it happened

that winter, there was a shiver of recognition
 followed by the chilly descent. An ambulance ride,
  then vision's thick return inside the emergency room's

hot breathy air. Memory's imperfection
 glimmering away. Falling is like that—
  the letting go, the scatter of moments suspended

until the body's brutal twist just before
 it disappears. One summer afternoon,
  my father climbed three flights

of his dormitory's fire escape. He leaned
  into warm paint, softened by the sun.
    One moment he was there, the next

he was falling. Did he remember
  the stunning backward drop, the instant
    of perfect sky when hard planks vanished

beneath his feet? Did all sensation shudder
  as his body scalded into the balmy air?
    Later that day, he climbed those stairs again.

Slower now, creeping, one leg wrapped
  to hold the bone that snapped when
    he landed. The crisscrossing boards

steadied his weight before his second dangerous
  trip into nothing. This fall was different,
    no safe landing imagined. His heavy leg

plunged him down, the rest of his body
  infinitely light before the breeze
    and quick drop. Did you experience

the same delicious tumble? All that winter,
  day after day, all thoughts of algebra,
    formulas, the lovely language of mathematics

smoothed from your worn-out head.
  You'd spill quietly over the linoleum floor,
    your arms and legs winding in careful disorder.

And later still, your head was carefully centered
   on a scratchy hospital pillow, covered
      in electrodes and patches to measure

your brain's dangerous skips. Nothing.
   There were never any answers. The one time
      you fell while knowing me, I arrived too late.

I stood beside your metal bed waiting
   for you to wake. *I don't remember anything,*
      you whispered, a dreamy glow still flushing

your face. Bruises gathered sweetly
   below your cheekbones. I leaned to taste your
      ruined mouth. Your eyes were patient, only

half awake when I said *Tell me how it feels*
   to fall. Tell me how
      to forget.

Beach Glass

What does the sea give back after water
has slipped away and then returned?
Is it beauty or mystery? I could add color
and detail until the tide disappears
on a tatter of lace and pearly foam.

This is the way it happens: we take a bus
to the end of the line, arrive in a coastal town
off-season. Empty, shuttered shops,
mute guesthouses closed for winter.
Down on the beach we inhale dampness

and salt, examine the sharp edges of beer bottles
and liquor jugs the sea has left behind.
Amber, cobalt, and colorless scraps shimmer
between rocks. It is dangerous. We follow
the glittering trail out to an island. We go inside

a summer shack where rotting boards sway,
every plank and knothole aching and swollen
from wet breezes. Splintered furniture leans
while water splashes outside. We embrace
under a doorframe, solid and whole.

I slide you to the floor, down to the old blanket
that smells of ruin, a thousand other mornings.
All day the gulls crash and moan over the rocks.
We match their lazy cries with our own, raise
our clothing, wait for the salty numbness.

I open and open. Half-dressed, shivering, we hope
for a storm to blow in across the thin slash of ocean.
Water begins to gather below the windows, the tide
coming up, stiff waves seeping back toward shore.
How much longer can we stay? I imagine all color vanishing,

sepia and ivory gone, our round bodies glossy with mist.
See how the water brings endless debris? Back on shore,
waves toss glass tokens all along the dark beach.
Each piece is rolled and smoothed to a dull finish,
each fragment a tiny jewel kindled by water.

In the Last Hour of Light

It could be any summer evening.
Mesh screens in upstairs windows
bulge with the day's last heat,
lean toward roses in the side yard.

In my parents' cool bedroom, my father
tosses rolled socks, dress shirts
still banded from the laundry, handkerchiefs—

a jumble of clothing and shaving soap
into a flat wide suitcase. He is crying,
tears skid off his cheeks onto a nest
of ties. My sister and I pull sleeves

from his suitcase, run back to his dresser, arms
full of nothing, pleading *don't go, don't go.*
He zips the case shut. Our voices travel relentless air,

glide easily out the windows and over the street
as we bump downstairs where Mother has passed out
on the new green couch. The screen door
knocks gently as sepia air lifts against

the house. Humidity and light blur
until my father sets his suitcase
on the worn bottom step and asks
in a new tarnished voice, *should I stay?*

Lessons

Mother carefully drew a small picture
one night, in pen on a blank
white sheet. *This is how a man is,*
she explained, then pointed, *and this
is a woman.* She threaded one fingertip
over sharp lines, not speaking of love
or passion, but dropped the paper on my bed.
Slowly I jumbled the shapes, forcing narrow

creases into paper, then smoothed it away
in a bureau drawer. Upstairs, through
the half-open door of their room, I saw them
making love in Dad's single bed. I'd been awakened
by a dream, and Mother's finely curved
back shivered white above his legs, both
moving in hushed ripples across pale bedcovers.
Even at that moment I knew to catch my softly

beating throat with stunned hands, afraid
my whispering pulse would wake us
all. I watched them mornings: bending
silent over eggs, the toast a little too
brown, doling newspaper sections before
work, never a word about anything. Years
later, when a man unbuttoned my blouse
with easy twists, his strange round mouth

tickling lazy kisses over my ears and
hair, I didn't wonder at our quiet.
Twisting beneath him to hold
the careful heartbeat inching along his neck,

I asked his name again. He smoothed his fine
dark body into me. In shifting
afternoon light he spoke one word
to the hollow center of my chest.

What Doesn't Go Away

On the back of a motorcycle, I leaned
into every highway curve. My body melted,
almost slipping face-first to gritty pavement
while holding him in my rapt arms. I argued
against the wind that rolled me toward asphalt,

but the air kissed me down, gluing my belly
to his polished back. You have to learn to bend.
When I watched my mother die, plastic tubes
removed, a quivering breath tossed her body
nearly upright. Bells rang, a signal

it was nearly over. When I was three,
I shook off her cold hand and slipped down
a snowpacked hill into traffic, smoothed
to a stop under a car paused at a light.
What I remember is chunked ice and salt

packed into every dull black curl of pipe
and machinery, small drips cascading
around frozen legs and arms, a snow angel underground.
It was perfectly still though my mother said she screamed
until the ambulance arrived. I could hear those soft drops

of water, dirt and salt mixed in, when it was very quiet,
even over the rasp of her infrequent pull for air.
It's what I turn to, the bend and gentle tickle
of the motor, even after the bells were turned off
and the nurse thumbed shut my mother's eyes.

Invocation

It is radar, of course,
though that's not
what I'm thinking
as the bat moves in the blueness

of this room. I know it likes to glide
the colorless air
and the filigreed webbing of stars
I watch through the ceiling's gash.
Little bits of glitter
foam down like confetti,

surrounding the torn mattress
where we try to sleep tonight.
Four nights here in this abandoned house,
refuge. Above my head the darkness
shimmers as the bat sails through the iced room.
My eyes are nearly used to the blackness,
the springs of the old mattress,
even used to you, still dressed in yesterday's

clothing. Above your sweet breath
I am awake, thinking of the bat's
easy orbit. It has night eyes.
They protect it from the roof's
crazy crossbeams and the kicked out walls
of discolored plaster. It floats on filaments
of light over silvery piles of old clothing

banked in every corner. See how it hovers,
love? So close we can surround it
with our chalky breath, no escape
within this borrowed room. Each time

the bat descends it pulls my hair
into blurry spirals. I wait. Listen
to its wings swing open as tufts of silk
tangle between the body and bone. I'm waiting
for you to feel the same soft brush of flight
across your sleep-dark face and see

the small beat of wings, your astonished body.
Fall deeper into the mattress with me. We'll watch
the bat rise and slip from this room. Watch it fly
above the roof into the embrace of dimmer stars
outside, the same dark blue sky that we can conjure
between us again and again
as the bat shudders a moment and is gone.

Viewing an Exhibition of Portraits by John Singer Sargent

In this darkened gallery the only real light
is from the unbelievable gleam off
the fawn, ecru, and ivory tinted Edwardian gowns.
See how they cluster, the pretty blooms of pale
fabrics, how they shimmer into sumptuous shades
of gold or perhaps a pinch of rose? My daughter

    is four. We're walking a hallway of borrowed
    paintings, admiring the dim billow of skirts,

the models' polished bodies trailing over plump divans.
These subjects in their intricate garments should not
hold her interest. I suppose she could easily
be in her own portrait with her pastel coloring
and the ashy hair my mother calls dirty dishwater
blonde. Sargent must have adored women,

    painting them in all their measured gestures.
    Clutching his palette of darks and lights, he waited

for the moment each subject devoured the pose and eased
into the cushions in a tangle of costume and revelatory expression.
I'm thinking of my mother and how even she wanted
that split second of illumination, the perfect scrap
of trembling light. It must have happened that summer
when she decided to be a platinum blonde. She destroyed

    color one afternoon, certain that each strand
    would blare white-hot. After mixing chemicals,

she turbaned her head in a wreath of foil. And waited.
She must have imagined the drama of white plumes,
feathers almost, the drop-dead ice cream whiteness,
all promised on the hair color box. But in her instant
of awareness, she was not glorified. Her hair was polished
strings and webs of tarnished silver. The color of old age—

    not the glimmering contagion of glamour. So what
    would she say about these society women on exhibit,

not a redhead or platinum blonde in sight? Just matrons
and their curious daughters, privileged little girls,
sisters with their sleek dark heads sharply angled.
All are graceful in the midst of elaborate floral
arrangements or when caught brushing one another's long
knotted hair. These are women who know beauty in each

    precise pose. My daughter moves toward a huge painting,
    skims past velvet ropes, reaches above the gilt frame.

One small hand adores the oils, the plumage,
the scrolling hem of the woman's frothy petticoat.
I don't pull her away. While she strokes the lavish
undergarment, I wonder what she's hoping to find.
Does she want their strange flowers and delicate clothing?
Does she touch the shimmering hues of faint color,

    the texture and glaze of paint, her own
    illumination and adornment still far away?

Acknowledgements

Grateful acknowledgment is made to the editors of the following publications in which some of these poems have appeared or are forthcoming:

Boulevard, Flint Hills Review, The Illinois Review, Interim, Poet Lore, The Prague Review, Puerto del Sol, and the anthologies *Fever Dreams: Contemporary Arizona Poetry* and *Dorothy Parker's Elbow: Tattoos on Writers, Writers on Tattoos.*

In the Fitting Room was selected for a prize by Marilyn Hacker in the Tucson International Poetry Festival XIII, March 1995.

It is a pleasure to thank my dear friends at the Ragdale Foundation for the time and space to work on these poems. And to Mark Doty, teacher, friend, my boundless gratitude for extraordinary support.

For specific and patient criticism, I thank Michael Carter, Jeremy Spears, and dearest of friends, Catherine Hammond. So many friends have helped me and I am especially grateful to Aaron Smith, Josie Kearns, Jimmy Berlin, Mark Wunderlich, Rick Noguchi, Martha Rhodes, Philip Mandel, Lois Roma-Deeley, Nancy Matte and Minnie Bruce Pratt.

For my first teacher, Chuck Aukema, and for Jack Pulaski, Paul Nelson, Cynthia Huntington, Gail Mazur, Roger Weingarten and Bruce Weigl.

To Jan Beatty for her passionate support, including my first wild radio interview. For believing in me before I knew, the late Marion Peterson. And for John Halonen, who has been there for all of this, relentless in his unwavering love.

About the Author

Virginia Chase Sutton is the recipient of numerous awards and honors for her writing including the Louis Untermeyer Scholar in Poetry at Bread Loaf, Allen Ginsberg Poetry Award and National Poet Hunt. Her poetry has appeared in Paris Review, Boulevard, Ploughshares, Witness, Antioch Review, and Western Humanities Review. A native of the Midwest, she lives in Arizona with her husband and two daughters. *Embellishments* is her first book of poetry.